Tucker

At The Ritz

by Linda Arst

illustrated by Sarah Tollin

Published by Sparkleberry Designs, LLC

ISBN 978-0-578-92832-6

For more information about this book visit our website:
www.tuckerattheritz.com

To my Maltese dog Tucker and his bestie, Shakti, who fill our hearts without trying!

To my family, who has been nothing but supportive in helping me finish this book.

To all the children I have had the pleasure of working with as an educator and the many life lessons you have taught me.

To all the kind and compassionate people who adopt rescue dogs and save lives.

Hot diggity dog!

Tucker is over the moon about his
vacation at the Ritz in sunny Florida. He
breaks into a happy dance when he sees
a special treat coming his way. It's a
ginormous peanut butter cookie,
wrapped with a big blue ribbon.

Every morning Tucker does a
splash dance at the beach.

"Surf's up!"

he howls. Then he grabs his surfboard
and rides the waves until he is dog-tired.

After resting for a bit, Tucker digs
a gigantic hole in the sand.
Suddenly, he discovers something
hard that feels like a shell. Uh-oh,
it's a crab that pinches his little
nose and won't let go.

"Woof-woof!"

yelps Tucker. "I have a sore sniffer!"

Tuesday mornings, Tucker bones up on his doga skills. The class begins with play-bows.

Downward dog is his most favorite pose.

Barking buddha is his second favorite. At the end of class, Tucker softly chants oms and finds his inner dogi.

Tucker spots a flying squirrel nearby and chases after it. He is flabbergasted when the squirrel glides 150 feet between trees. Tucker feels so foolish when he ends the chase barking up the wrong tree.

The Pilates for Pups class is next on Tucker's schedule. Puppy push-ups always make his tummy muscles sore. The treadmill is

super-fun

because Tucker can run as fast as a jackrabbit!

Tucker zips over to the Doggie Dash
& Dawdle race to help raise money
for homeless cats and dogs.

He wins first place and is
proud to be crowned Top Dog!

DOGGIE DASH & DAWDLE

Tucker celebrates at the Pooch-A-Palooza Carnival. He bobs for cheese, makes paw print art and gives out doggie kisses.

This is truly Tucker's Lucky Dog Day!

Tucker wakes up dog-hungry from his cat nap. He does the Kibble Dance by wagging his tail and shaking his tush. Then, he scarfs down a whole bowl of food and sprints over to the Happy Tails Dog Park for

Yappy Hour!

Tucker hops on a skateboard. He whizzes by the swings and bounces off a rock.

"Ouch!" he shrieks.

Tucker lands with a big bang and has bumps and bruises everywhere. His besties, Shakti, Cooper, Pickles and Fred rush over to see if he is hurt. "I am A-OK," whimpers Tucker. "Next time, I'll be sure to wear my helmet and knee pads!

Five Maltese puppies have just arrived
with their nanny and they are all

ankle-biters!

Everyone has to keep an eye on
them, including Tucker!

Tucker is all

tuckered out

after his play date, so he heads to the Posh
Paws Spa for a sports massage, blueberry
facial and pawdicure. He relaxes by
listening to Mozart and Beethoven.

Tucker is a little embarrassed when he
catches himself howling to the music.
Other dogs start howling and it turns into
a happy howl-fest!

Chilling out at the pool is one of Tucker's favorite things to do. He loves the cinnamon bun bites and carob cruncher treats. They keep his tail wagging all afternoon. Suddenly, Tucker yells,

"holy guacamole!"

A giant green iguana is sprinting toward him. Tucker thinks, "Whew, that was a close call. Luckily, iguanas like to eat plants and flowers, not dogs!"

Thursday is Tucker's Day to volunteer at the Wiggle Waggles dog shelter. He greets all the new dogs with a special gift basket of homemade peanut butter and bacon glazed treats. They are

barkalicious!

Toodle Lou is one of Tucker's best buddies and she is leaving Wiggle Waggles to be adopted by a loving family. Tucker was adopted, too, so he appreciates how lucky dogs are to be loved. He will miss Toodle Lou oodles and oodles, but they will be

furever friends!

Back at the Ritz, Tucker is out
on the balcony and spots some

awesome kites

flying high in the sky.

The gigantic clownfish is his favorite.

He wishes he could sail way up in the air with it.

Tucker writes a poem about the clownfish.

Its bright orange color makes him smile!

See the Clownfish soaring in the sky.

Tail waving in the wind

Way up high.

Hey Mr. Clownfish

With your big fin.

Looks like you're smiling

A great big grin!

"Oh phooey!" grumbles Tucker. "All my treats are gone." Tucker jogs down to the Wagging Tails store for a shopping spree. His friends, Benny, Cece, and Marvin are there at doggie training classes. Tucker joins them and does his roll over trick. He is rewarded with an Apple Crunch Pupcake that is

yummy in his tummy!

Tucker stops at

Starpups

on his way back to the Ritz. He has been craving a Puppuccino from their secret menu. It's a cup of whipped cream made especially for dogs. Charlie, a Chow Chow, is eyeing the Puppuccino and making grumpy growling sounds.

Tucker finishes his treat and skedaddles out of there!

After a long day, it's bath time.

Splish, splash,

Tucker's bubble bath is so much fun. Toot, his rubber duckie, goes into the tub with him. Water squirts from Toot's beak and gets everyone soaking wet.

Tucker dries off by shaking from the tip of his nose to the tip of his tail. He yips, barks and yodels. Then, he gets

the zoomies

and races around the room as fast as a speeding train.

At bed time, Tucker is a little snuggle puppy. He tidies up his toys, brushes his teeth, and gives everyone hugs and kisses. Tucker is pawsitively exhausted. He can't wait to hop into his bed that is fit for a king. Bailey, his favorite toy bunny, curls up with him.

"Sweet dreams,"

Tucker whispers to Bailey.

Continue the fun with Tucker's favorite recipe and game!

Apple Crunch Pupcakes
So doggone delicious!

Ingredients

2 3/4 cups water
1/4 cup applesauce
1/8 teaspoon vanilla
1 egg

2 tablespoons honey
4 cups whole wheat flour
1 cup chopped apple
1 tablespoon baking powder

Directions

Preheat oven to 350 degrees. Mix water, applesauce, vanilla, egg and honey together. Combine flour, apple and baking powder. Add wet ingredients to dry and mix thoroughly. Coat the muffin pan with vegetable spray and spoon in the mixture. Bake at 350 degrees for approximately 35 minutes. **Poochilicious!**

Shadow Matching Game

Have a grown-up cut out the picture cards. Mix them up and place them face down. Flip over two cards and see if you can match the shape of a shadow with its colorful picture. If they match, keep the cards. If they don't, return the cards face down. Players take turns and whoever has the most cards wins!

Thank you so much for reading Tucker's story. I hope you had a fun time. If so, please help others enjoy it and leave a review on Amazon.

Fun and printable games!

Stay up to date with Tucker's dog-loving adventures by visiting these sites.

www.tuckerattheritz.com

Facebook.com/lindabarst

https://www.instagram.com/tuckerattheritz/

Made in the USA
Middletown, DE
09 May 2022

65380937R00031